T0407394

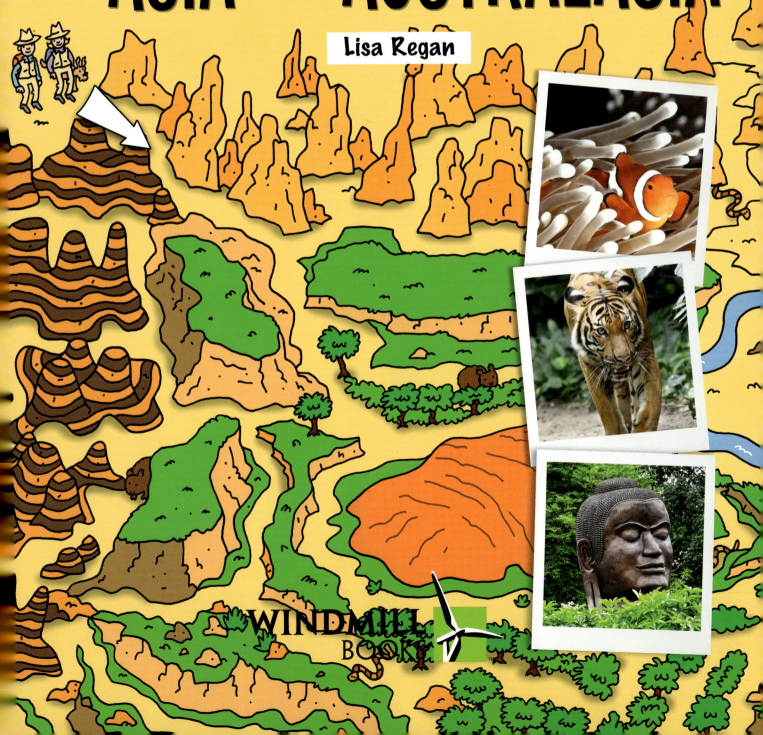

A-MAZE-ING
ADVENTURES

A-MAZE-ING ADVENTURES IN ASIA AND AUSTRALASIA

Lisa Regan

WINDMILL
BOOKS

Are you ready... for the adventure of a lifetime?

Join us, Max, Millie, and our pet dog, Mojo, on a trip to see amazing and exciting sights! Everywhere we go, we'll need your help. Use your finger to help us solve the tricky mazes. Along the way, we'll find hidden objects and learn some fascinating facts. We're going to take lots of photographs and make notes as we go.

Published in 2021 by Windmill Books, an Imprint of Rosen Publishing 29 East 21st Street, New York, NY 10010

Copyright © Arcturus Holdings Ltd, 2021

Cataloging-in-Publication Data

Names: Regan, Lisa.
Title: A-maze-ing adventures in Asia and Australasia / Lisa Regan.
Description: New York : Windmill Books, 2021. | Series: A-maze-ing adventures | Includes glossary and index.
Identifiers: ISBN 9781499485530 (pbk.) | ISBN 9781499485554 (library bound) | ISBN 9781499485547 (6 pack) | ISBN 9781499485561 (ebook)
Subjects: LCSH: Maze puzzles--Juvenile literature. | Asia--Juvenile literature. | Australasia--Juvenile literature.
Classification: LCC GV1507.M3 P484 2021 | DDC 793.73'8--dc23

Manufactured in the United States of America

CPSIA Compliance Information: Batch BS20WM: For Further Information contact Rosen Publishing, New York, New York at 1-800-237-9932

Find us on

Contents

Welcome to Asia 4

Dragon Dance 6

Great Wall 8

Man-Made Wonders 10

Head for Heights 12

Rainy Season 14

Ring of Fire 16

Welcome to Australasia 18

Down Under 20

City Sights 22

Kangaroo Island 24

Kia Ora! 26

Answers 28

Glossary 30

Further Information 31

Index 32

Ted the ginger cat is going to tag along. He goes everywhere we go, but he's very shy, so he'll be hiding most of the time. See if you can find him in each maze!

Welcome to

ASIA

Asia is the world's largest continent! We're starting in the east, in China, with its dragons, busy cities, and the Great Wall. From there, it's across to the United Arab Emirates and then up Mount Everest in the massive Himalayas. When we come back down, we'll zoom across to Vietnam and the Philippines, which are watery places with beautiful religious and historic sights to see.

NORTH AMERICA

EUROPE

ASIA

AFRICA

SOUTH AMERICA

AUSTRALASIA

RUSSIA

KAZAKHSTAN

MONGOLIA

START

TURKEY

IRAQ

IRAN

CHINA

JAPAN

PAKISTAN

NEPAL

SAUDI
ARABIA

UNITED
ARAB
EMIRATES

INDIA

YEMEN

FINISH

CAMBODIA

PHILIPPINES

MALAYSIA

VIETNAM

INDONESIA

Dragon Dance

It's time to celebrate! We are in China for the Spring Festival. Teams of dancers carry dragon costumes and perform in the streets to celebrate the arrival of a new year.

FACT FILE

COUNTRY: China
CONTINENT: Asia
CAPITAL CITY: Beijing

China has more people living there than any other country. It is also one of the biggest countries and contains deserts and mountains, subtropical forests, and huge grassland areas. The people live mostly in the eastern side of the country. Their New Year celebrations take place in January or February, when small gifts are exchanged and firecrackers are set off to scare away evil spirits.

Red envelopes with money inside bring good luck.

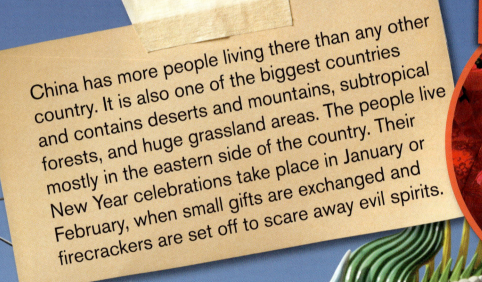

dancing dragon

Help our friends dance their way through the performers without getting thrown off course.

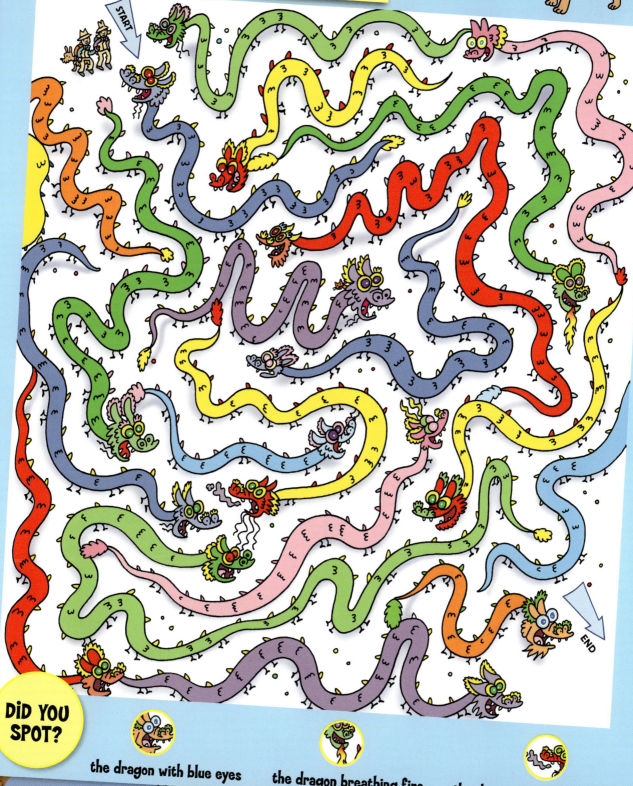

START

END

Great Wall

We've taken a trip to the north of China to see the Great Wall, built thousands of years ago to keep out dangerous invaders and control who was allowed into the country.

FACT FILE

COUNTRY: China
CONTINENT: Asia
CAPITAL CITY: Beijing

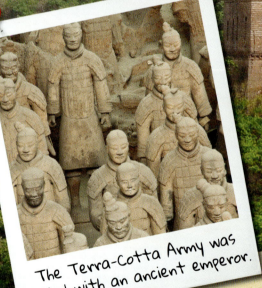

The Terra-Cotta Army was buried with an ancient emperor.

The Great Wall runs from east to west near the northern border of China. It was built in separate sections for several different emperors. The people who built it were usually criminals, captured enemies, and slaves, and were not paid. It was constructed over so many centuries that it is a mixture of mud, grass, stone, bricks, and wood. The towers were sentry posts and provided shelter and storage.

This should be called the Long and Winding Wall! Try to find a path to the main tower at the end.

START

END

DID YOU SPOT?

5 peeking pandas

2 Chinese dragons

the Ming vase

9

Man-Made Wonders

We are living it up in one of the wealthiest countries in the world, the United Arab Emirates. Time for some sun, sea, and luxury shopping!

FACT FILE

COUNTRY: United Arab Emirates
CONTINENT: Asia
CAPITAL CITY: Abu Dhabi

The United Arab Emirates, or UAE, is a country on the Arabian Peninsula, next to the Persian Gulf. It is made up of seven emirates. Dubai is famous for its skyscrapers and luxury hotels. The Burj Khalifa skyscraper opened in 2010 as the tallest building in the world. The man-made Palm Islands are also in Dubai. They are shaped like palm trees and are made from sand pumped from the ocean floor.

The Burj Khalifa contains offices and apartments.

Swim with dolphins in Dubai!

Explore these amazing islands by boating through the channels between them and heading for shore.

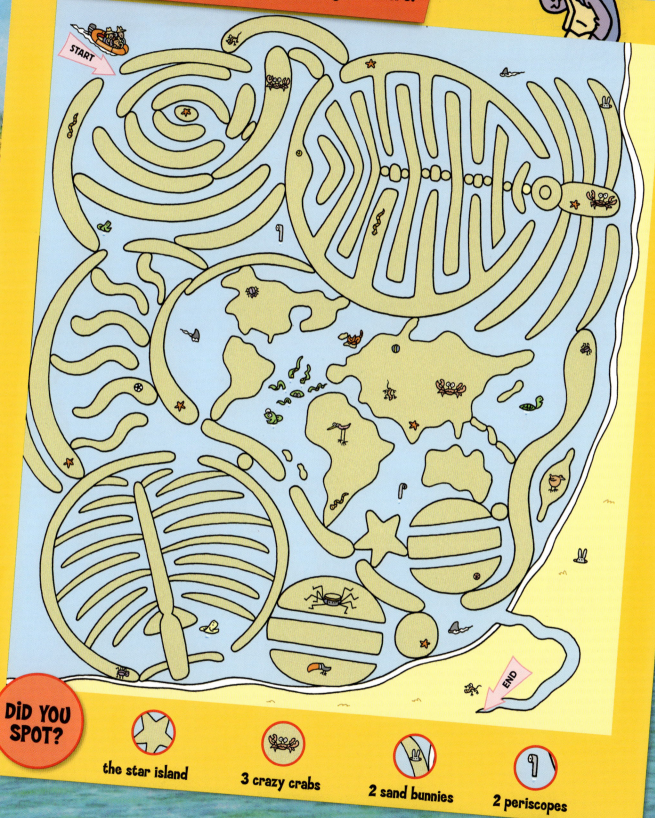

START

END

DID YOU SPOT?

the star island

3 crazy crabs

2 sand bunnies

2 periscopes

11

Head for Heights

We are on top of the world! We are in the Nepalese part of the Himalaya mountain range, which contains eight of the world's ten tallest peaks.

FACT FILE

COUNTRY: Nepal
CONTINENT: Asia
CAPITAL CITY: Kathmandu

The Himalaya mountain range passes through five countries: Nepal, Bhutan, India, China, and Pakistan. It contains the highest mountain in the world, Mount Everest. Climbers can choose whether to start their Everest ascent from North Base Camp in Tibet, part of China, or South Base Camp in Nepal. The beautiful but endangered snow leopard can be found in these mountains.

Yaks often carry supplies for Everest climbers.

Find a way down the snowy slopes for Max, Millie, and Mojo. They're following in the footsteps of the mysterious Yeti!

START

END

DID YOU SPOT?

the werewolf

a pair of Yeti slippers

the unicorn

3 dead trees

Rainy Season

Next stop, Vietnam, a long, narrow country covered in hills and forests. Like the rest of Southeast Asia, it suffers from heavy seasonal rains called monsoons.

FACT FILE

COUNTRY: Vietnam
CONTINENT: Asia
CAPITAL CITY: Hanoi

The Indochinese tiger can be found in Vietnam.

Vietnam has a very wet climate with two monsoons a year, which is why many people live in floating villages (pictured). The nation was isolated from the rest of the world by the Vietnam War (1955–1975), but now it has good relations with most countries. During the war, the locals used a lengthy tunnel system for hiding and storage. These Cu Chi tunnels are now a tourist attraction.

Find a way out of the secret tunnels without bumping into the scary giant spiders!

END

START

DID YOU SPOT?

7 scary spiders

8 lanterns

the cave troll

the secret radio

15

Ring of Fire

We have made it to the Philippines. This country is a string of islands. The proper name for this is an archipelago. The Chocolate Hills (pictured) turn brown in the dry season, like chocolate!

The Philippines are located on the Pacific Ring of Fire, an area in the Pacific where many earthquakes and volcanic eruptions happen. Farmers cut terraces, like large steps, into the sides of slopes to make use of the land. They are watered by an irrigation system from the rain forests high above. The stepped fields keep in the water, instead of it flowing straight to the bottom. Some rice terraces here are 2,000 years old!

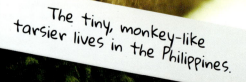

The tiny, monkey-like tarsier lives in the Philippines.

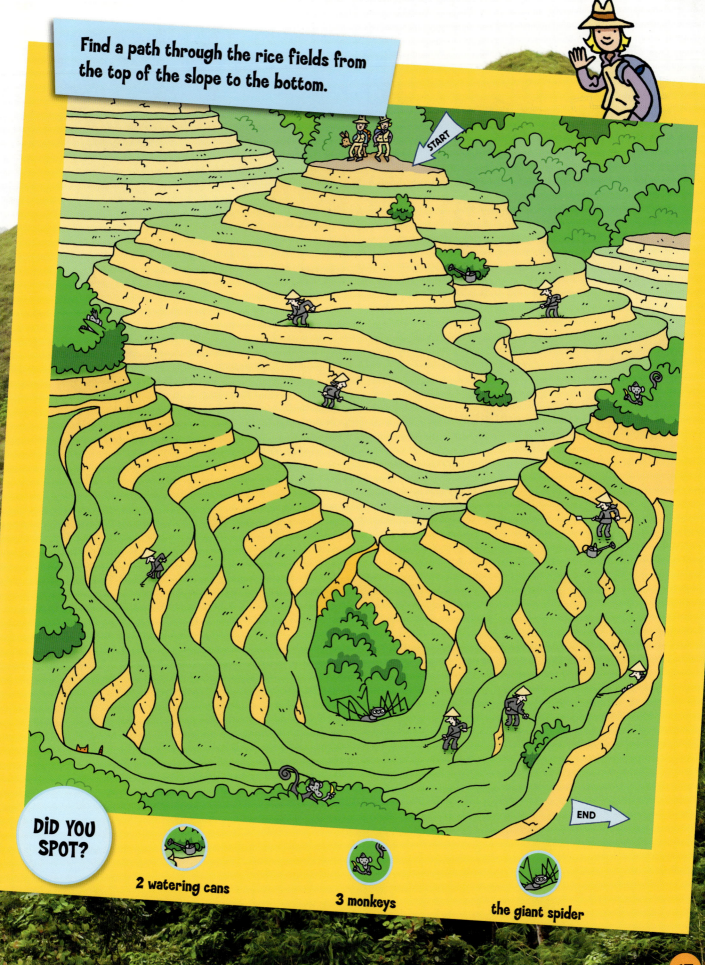

Find a path through the rice fields from the top of the slope to the bottom.

START

END

DID YOU SPOT?

2 watering cans

3 monkeys

the giant spider

Welcome to
AUSTRALASIA

There's so much to see in Australasia!
We're off down under to see Australia's
hot, dry Outback, and its coasts and busy cities.
From the mainland, we'll hop over to see the
wildlife on Kangaroo Island. Then it's
over the sea to New Zealand, where we're
staying on the amazing North Island.
It's so exciting!

PAPUA
NEW
GUINEA

SOLOMON
ISLANDS

AUSTRALIA

START

NEW
CALEDONIA

FINISH

TASMANIA

NEW
ZEALAND

Down Under

We are in Australia, a land of extremes. In this one country, you can find desert, rain forest, farmland, and even places permanently covered in snow.

FACT FILE

COUNTRY: Australia
CONTINENT: Australia
CAPITAL: Canberra

Most people in Australia live in or near its ten largest cities, mainly around the eastern and southeastern coasts. Canberra was built in 1908 to serve as the country's capital. Inland, the terrain becomes drier and rockier. It is hard for people to survive in these central areas, known as the Bush and the Outback, so few people live there, but these distinctive landscapes are home to animals native only to Australia—red kangaroos, emus, koalas, and dingoes.

NEXT 10 km

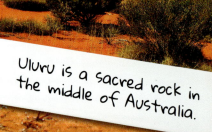

Uluru is a sacred rock in the middle of Australia.

DID YOU SPOT?

4 snakes

5 wombats

2 wallabies

2 sleeping crocs

City Sights

Welcome to Sydney! It's not Australia's capital, but it's the country's largest and oldest city, with friendly people, great beaches, and lots to see.

FACT FILE

COUNTRY: Australia
CONTINENT: Australia
CITY: Sydney

One of Sydney's most famous sights is the inspirational Opera House, designed in the 1950s to look like shells sticking out of the water. It contains two main opera halls, but about 1,000 rooms altogether. It took six years longer and cost ten times more to build than originally planned! For a different view of the city, you can climb right over the railings of the Sydney Harbour Bridge (pictured) on a guided tour.

Bondi Beach is a popular tourist spot in Sydney.

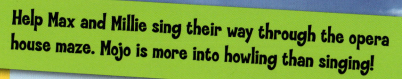

Help Max and Millie sing their way through the opera house maze. Mojo is more into howling than singing!

START

END

DID YOU SPOT?

3 opera bunnies · the super soprano · the giant spider · the bemused fish

Kangaroo Island

We're going to leave mainland Australia now and explore Kangaroo Island, which is just off Australia's south coast, across the sea from the city of Adelaide.

FACT FILE

COUNTRY: Australia
CONTINENT: Australia
PLACE: Kangaroo Island

This small island is a wildlife haven. If you want to see Australian animals, then come here! The island is teeming with kangaroos, koalas and wallabies, but you may also catch a glimpse of something rarer, such as the echidna, which is also sometimes known as the spiny anteater. Don't forget to join in the Kangaroo Island wave, a friendly custom of raising your first finger to any cars that drive past!

Island koalas are causing problems by eating too much.

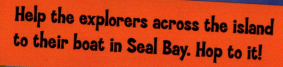

Help the explorers across the island to their boat in Seal Bay. Hop to it!

DID YOU SPOT?

4 sneaky sharks

5 cool koalas

4 pleased pelicans

the happy turtle

25

Kia Ora!

This means "Welcome to New Zealand!" It is so far from other land that it was one of the last places to have humans living there.

FACT FILE

COUNTRY: New Zealand
REGION: Australasia
CAPITAL CITY: Wellington

New Zealand is made up of two main islands, North and South. North Island has the country's capital city, Wellington, and its largest city, Auckland (pictured), home to the Sky Tower. It also has geothermal sites where you can see bubbling mud pools, smell the stinky-egg gases leaking out of the ground, and bathe in the naturally warm waters. The native Maori people still cook food in the steam for tourists to eat.

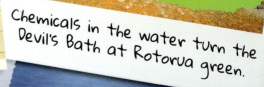

Chemicals in the water turn the Devil's Bath at Rotorua green.

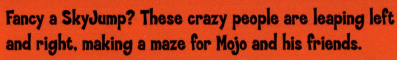

Fancy a SkyJump? These crazy people are leaping left and right, making a maze for Mojo and his friends.

DID YOU SPOT?

the giant spider   the shy gorilla   the superhero   3 brown birds

Answers

6–7 Dragon Dance

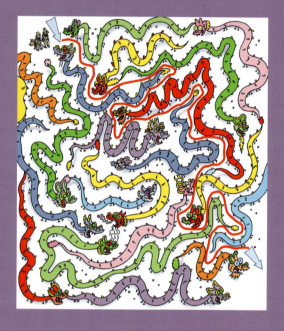

8–9 Great Wall

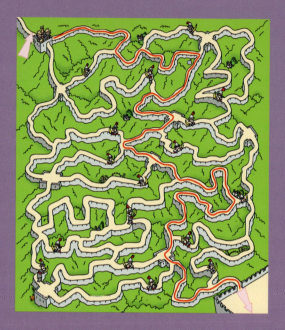

10–11 Man-Made Wonders

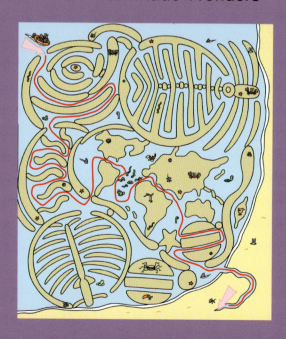

12–13 Head for Heights

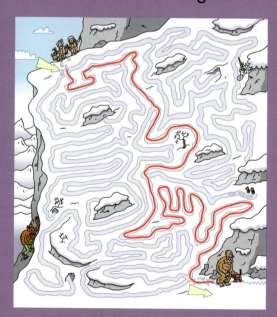

14–15   Rainy Season

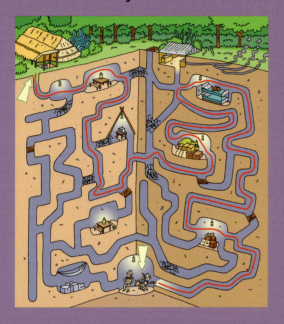

16–17   Ring of Fire

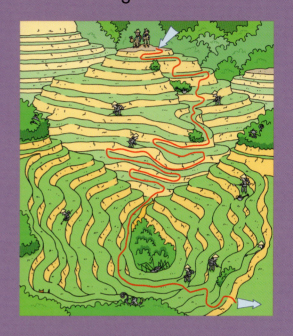

20–21   Down Under

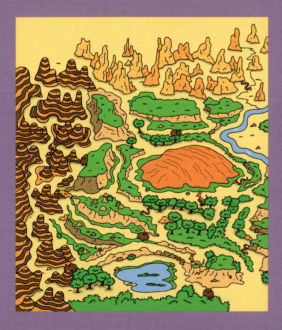

22–23   City Sights

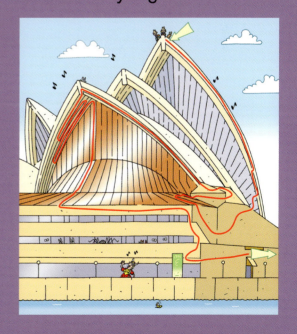

24–25 Kangaroo Island

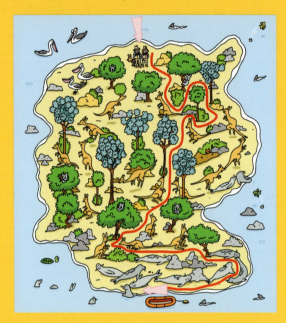

26–27 Kia Ora!

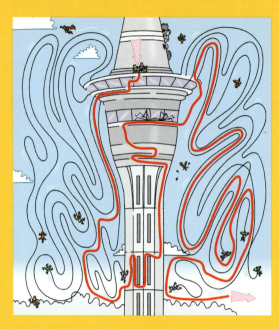

Glossary

archipelago A large group of islands.

Australasia An area that includes Australia, New Zealand, and other surrounding islands.

continent Any of the world's seven main landmasses.

emirate Land or a region ruled over by an emir.

endangered At risk of extinction.

firecrackers Small, explosive fireworks.

geothermal Warmth that comes from the internal heat of Earth.

monsoon A season of heavy rains in South and Southeast Asia.

native People, animals, or plants that come from or are found in a specific place.

subtropical Regions that are close to tropical regions (tropical regions are close to the equator).

Further Information

Books

Asia / Australia (Go Exploring! Continents and Oceans)
by Steffi Cavel-Clarke, BookLife Publishing, 2017

Children's Picture Atlas Usborne, 2003

Mapping Asia / Australasia and Antarctica (Close-Up Continents)
by Paul Rockett, Franklin Watts, 2016

The Travel Book: A Journey Through Every Country in the World
Lonely Planet Kids, 2017

Websites

www.google.com/earth

Explore the world in stunning satellite imagery.

www.natgeokids.com/za/category/discover/geography

National Geographic Kids has a wealth of information
on animals and countries.

Publisher's note to educators and parents: Our editors have carefully reviewed these websites to ensure that they are suitable for students. Many websites change frequently, however, and we cannot guarantee that a site's future contents will continue to meet our high standards of quality and educational value. Be advised that students should be closely supervised whenever they access the Internet.

Index

animals 10, 12, 14, 16, 20, 24
Australia 18, 19, 20–25

Burj Khalifa (skyscraper) 10

China 4, 5, 6–7, 8–9, 12
cities 4, 18, 20, 22–23, 26
    Auckland, New Zealand 26
    Canberra, Australia 20
    Dubai, United Arab Emirates 10
    Sydney, Australia 22–23

deserts 6, 20

farmland 16, 20
forests 6, 14

Great Wall of China 4, 8–9

islands 10, 11, 16, 18, 19, 24, 25, 26

Kangaroo Island 18, 19, 24–25

Maori people 26
maps 4, 5, 18, 19
monsoons 14

mountains 4, 6, 12
Mount Everest 4, 12

Nepal 5, 12–13
New Zealand 18, 19, 26–27

Philippines 4, 5, 16–17

rain forests 16, 20

snow 12, 13, 20

Uluru, Australia 20
United Arab Emirates (UAE)
    4, 5, 10–11

Vietnam 4, 5, 14–15